NATIONAL GEOGRAPHIC

Ladders

THE INCA
Pre-Columbian Americans

WHO WERE THE INCA?

by Andrea Alter

Mysterious. Brilliant. Powerful. These words describe the Inca, a civilization that lived in South America before Columbus came to the Americas. The Inca emerged as a mountain culture in central Peru around the year A.D. 1100. In only a few hundred years, they'd built an empire that extended 2,500 miles and ruled 12 million people. Their quick rise amazes historians. It might amaze you, too!

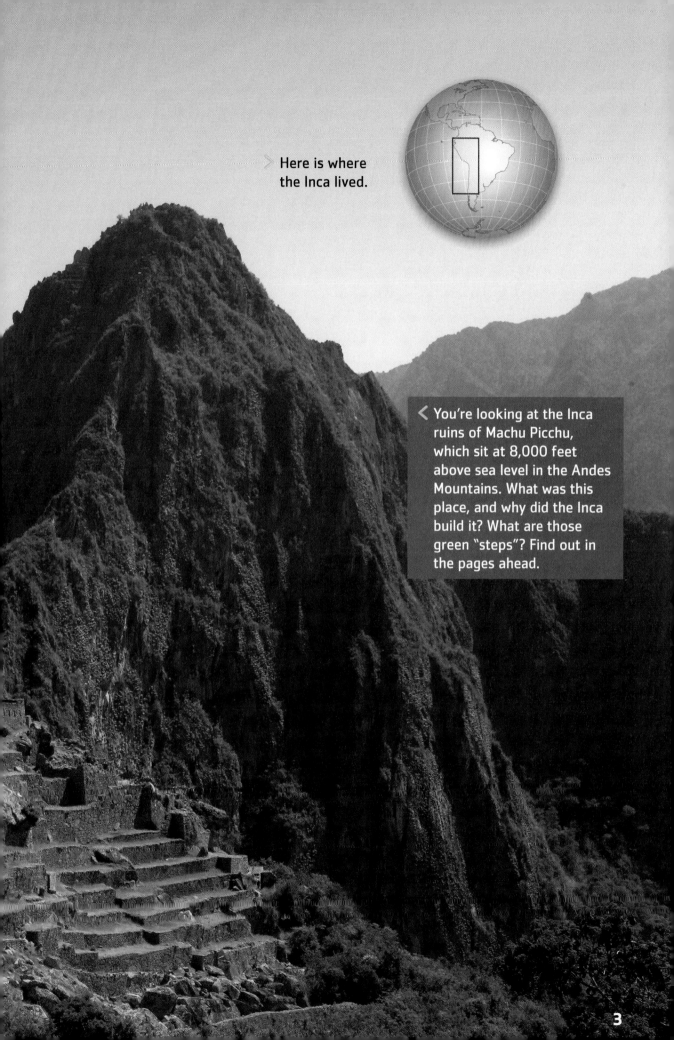

> Here is where the Inca lived.

< You're looking at the Inca ruins of Machu Picchu, which sit at 8,000 feet above sea level in the Andes Mountains. What was this place, and why did the Inca build it? What are those green "steps"? Find out in the pages ahead.

THE EMPIRE BUILDERS

To get a sense of why the Inca amaze us, let's start in the mountain range where they lived. The Andes are some of the highest mountains in the world, and they extend the length of the western side of South America. Peaks of more than 20,000 feet overlook deep gorges, or steep canyons. This wasn't the easiest place to build a large empire.

The mountainous land didn't discourage the Inca, though. In a short period of time, a series of Inca rulers built an empire by overpowering neighboring groups, sometimes by force. At its height, the Inca Empire included parts of present-day Colombia, Ecuador, Peru, Bolivia, Chile, and Argentina.

How did the Inca manage such a large empire? First, Inca society was highly organized. At the top, Inca emperors were considered **descendants**, or relatives, of the Inca sun god. Families belonged to larger kinship groups, and these groups shared land and worked together. Everyone, in some way, worked for the empire—whether road building, farming, making pottery, or mining for gold and silver.

To connect distant villages and cities, the Inca built stone roads and trails and as many as 200 suspension bridges—bridges of rope that hang above impassable rivers and gorges. Quick communication also strengthened the empire. Runners relayed messages and kept the Inca connected, sometimes covering 140 miles in a day.

The Inca built a powerful empire in only a few hundred years. But would it last?

As you can see, the Inca built their empire quickly. In less than 150 years, the Inca Empire stretched nearly the length of the South American continent.

BUILDING AN EMPIRE

1 1400

The Inca lived in the Urubamba (oo-roo-VAHM-bah) Valley. The Inca began their expansion around 1400.

2 1470

By 1470, the Inca had reached the coast and extended their power northward into present-day Ecuador.

3 1500

By 1500, the Inca had expanded as far south as present-day Chile. They united their vast empire using more than 14,000 miles of roads.

4 1532

The Inca reached the eastern slope of the Andes in the 1530s. By 1532, the Inca Empire included more than 300,000 square miles and 12 million people.

Inca Roads ═══

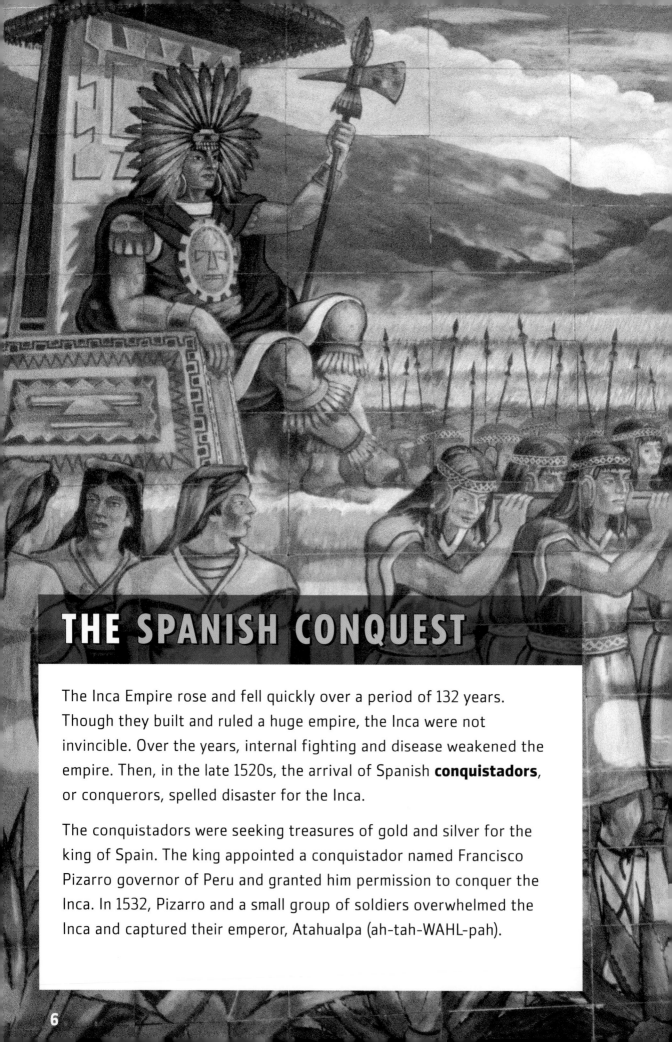

THE SPANISH CONQUEST

The Inca Empire rose and fell quickly over a period of 132 years. Though they built and ruled a huge empire, the Inca were not invincible. Over the years, internal fighting and disease weakened the empire. Then, in the late 1520s, the arrival of Spanish **conquistadors**, or conquerors, spelled disaster for the Inca.

The conquistadors were seeking treasures of gold and silver for the king of Spain. The king appointed a conquistador named Francisco Pizarro governor of Peru and granted him permission to conquer the Inca. In 1532, Pizarro and a small group of soldiers overwhelmed the Inca and captured their emperor, Atahualpa (ah-tah-WAHL-pah).

∨ Upon meeting, Pizarro and his soldiers captured Atahualpa and held him for ransom. Here, Pizarro confronts Atahualpa, who wears a pendant that depicts the Inca sun god.

Soon after, the Inca capital, Cusco (KOO-skoh), fell. The Spanish established a new capital at Lima in 1535. The Inca Empire had come to an end.

What happened to the Inca after the Spanish conquest? Life was definitely different, and Inca culture changed dramatically. The Inca had to learn the Spanish language. Some Inca fled to high mountains or the jungles of the Amazon Basin. Others remained and became laborers under Spanish rule.

While life changed for the Inca, their influence remained. The Inca left behind beautiful artifacts and structures. Later generations have marveled at the skill and brilliance of the Inca.

INFLUENCE OF THE INCA TODAY

Since the 1500s, Inca culture has been passed down among the descendants of the Inca, the Quechua (KECH-wah). The Quechua are an **indigenous**, or native, people in South America. Most Quechua live in the mountains of Peru, but some live in Bolivia and Ecuador. They maintain their traditional culture through their language, religion, farming, and art.

The language the Quechua speak is also called *Quechua*. To keep the Quechua language from disappearing in today's world, educators in Peru want to increase Quechua language instruction, especially where Quechua children go to school.

Farming techniques have not changed much in this region since the time of the Inca. The Quechua grow potatoes and other crops on **terraces**, or raised fields cut into the mountainsides. As they did for the Inca, these terraces create flat fields in which to plant crops, and they capture rainwater that would otherwise just flow off the rocky mountain slopes.

Like the Inca did, the Quechua raise sheep, llamas, and alpacas for wool. They collect the wool, spin it, and dye it to form vibrant yarns. Skilled Quechua artisans then weave the yarns into blankets, shawls, scarves, bags, and ponchos (PON-chohs). Their weavings often feature animals, plants, birds, and insects in traditional designs that connect the Quechua to the Inca culture of the past.

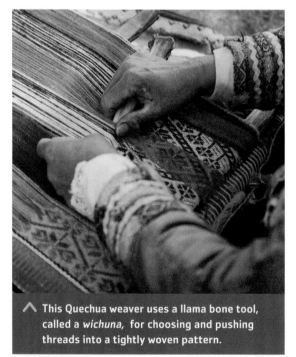

∧ This Quechua weaver uses a llama bone tool, called a *wichuna,* for choosing and pushing threads into a tightly woven pattern.

This Quechua student's uniform reflects his culture's traditional dress. Quechua schoolchildren in Peru learn Quechua and Spanish.

Check In Where and when did the Inca live, and who are their descendants today?

LLAND of the LLAMA

by Sheri Reda

To most people, llamas are cute and curious-looking animals with heavy-lidded eyes and goofy smiles, so you might not realize how important they were to the Inca Empire. The Inca tended huge herds of llamas. They wove images of llamas into their cloth and even buried their dead with golden llama figurines. The Inca honored llamas because they depended on these strong, woolly creatures in many ways.

Without llamas, it would have been difficult for the Inca to travel around their mountain empire. The Inca lacked wheeled vehicles, but they didn't need them. They had llamas to transport them and their goods over their wide-ranging system of roads. For example, Inca builders used llamas to carry heavy loads such as stones and other building materials over rugged terrain.

Inca farmers used llamas to carry water to their fields and collected llama dung, or waste, to use as fertilizer for crops and fuel for fires. They gathered llama wool and wove it into beautiful blankets and cloaks. When a llama died, its fat was used to make candles, its hide was used to make leather, and its meat provided extra nutrition for the hardworking Inca. Llamas just might be one of the most useful animals around.

Llamas can live and work in high mountain regions.

Cool Things About Llamas

You might not guess by looking at them, but llamas are close relatives of camels. Even though they don't have humps, llamas are in fact one of four camel relatives that live in South America—the others are alpacas, vicuñas (vih-KOON-yuhz), and guanacos (gwuh-NAH-kohz). Llamas are perfectly suited to live high up in the Andes Mountains. Want to know why? Let's hear the answers straight from the llama's mouth.

Hello, llama fans! I bet I can guess what you want to ask me. "Do I spit?" Llamas have gotten a bad rap about this habit thanks to our camel relatives. But we don't spit unless we're mad or threatened. And we don't often get mad at humans. If we DO get mad, watch out . . .

Some of us wear ear tags for identification, not for decoration. There's no reason to decorate our beautiful, banana-shaped ears. Ear shape is one way to tell us apart from our alpaca relatives. They have straight ears. Boring!

My fine, downy undercoat keeps me soft, warm, and cuddly. The wool of my undercoat is so soft, cozy, and beautiful that people use it to make blankets and clothing.

You only have one stomach? Poor you! My three stomachs help me digest the grass and shrubs I love to munch, so I can go long distances without stopping to eat or drink. I can go for days without water, though not as long as my camel cousins in Asia.

My feet are made for mountain climbing. My two big toes help me balance on steep, uneven soil. My soles are tough and leathery to protect my feet from rocky trails, and my hooves are perfectly formed for climbing the rocky Andean mountainsides.

My coarse guard hair, which I wear over my undercoat, protects me from moisture and dirt. It's just an old overcoat, but people love it. I don't mind if folks take some from time to time. I can always grow more.

Not only am I adorable, but I am also supercharged. My blood has more kinds of red blood cells than most other mammals, and these cells help carry oxygen quickly and easily throughout my body. That gives me energy for the long haul, even high in the mountains where the air doesn't have much oxygen.

13

Woolly and Warm

When it comes to wool, llamas get a two-for-one deal. Their soft undercoat protects them against extreme cold or heat. Their second coat, which is made of a type of hair called guard hair, repels moisture and dirt, keeping llamas—and people wearing llama wool—comfortable and dry. That's the practical part of llama wool. The pretty part is that llama wool comes in several natural colors, including black, dark brown, reddish brown, white, and gray. And unlike sheep's wool, it doesn't shrink in the wash.

To get the wool off a llama, farmers first remove dust and dirt from the llama. Some farmers use wire brushes, while others use leaf blowers. Then they **shear**, or shave off, the wool, leaving a little behind to keep the llama warm. Most farmers today shear their llamas with electric clippers. More traditional farmers use a sharp knife. That might sound scary, but it's just an old-fashioned haircut like barbers used to give. It doesn't hurt the llama at all, and the shearer ends up with five to twenty pounds of wool.

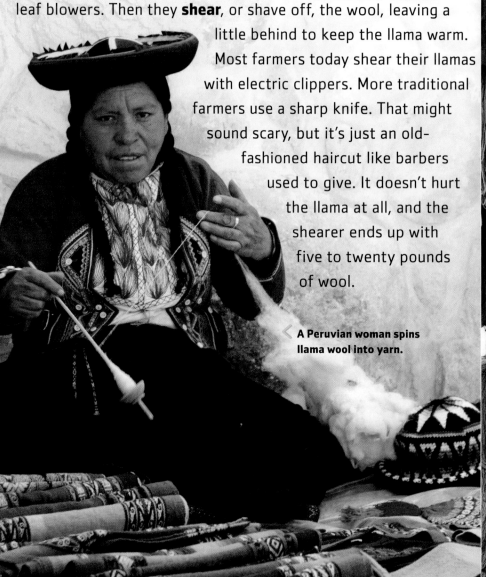

A Peruvian woman spins llama wool into yarn.

Leaves, roots, and bug bodies are ground into powder to make dyes. These dyes give llama yarn its brilliant colors.

It takes a few more steps to turn a pile of llama wool into a beautiful **textile**. A textile is a piece of cloth or woven fabric. Llama wool can be dyed a variety of colors, including a traditional bright red color made from female cochineal (KAH-chuh-neel) insects. Most dyes are made with natural materials, such as different types of plants.

Craftspeople spin the wool into yarn. Then they knit the yarn into jackets and other garments, twist the yarn into rope, or weave it to make cloth or rugs. Artists use it to create beautiful wall hangings, prized around the world. Leave it to a llama to offer usefulness, beauty, and comfort, all at once.

A merchant sells colorful llama yarn at this market in Peru.

Check In   How have llamas adapted to life in the Andes Mountains?

15

A Tour of Machu Picchu

by Mary Peake

Would you like to visit one of the world's most fascinating historical sites? Then lace up your hiking boots and let's travel to Machu Picchu (MAH-choo PEE-choo).

Machu Picchu—the name means "old peak"—was a small Inca city built in the 1400s. Perched high in the Andes Mountains, the site overlooks the Urubamba River Valley, also known as the Sacred Valley. Hidden away in the mountains, 70 miles from the capital of the Inca Empire, Machu Picchu's **remote** location helped preserve it. For hundreds of years, the world did not know it existed.

How do you get to Machu Picchu? The easy way is to take a train from the city of Cusco, Peru. The hard way is to hike the 28-mile Inca Trail that winds up from the Urubamba River to the historic site. Some people take four days to hike the whole trail, and others start midway up for a two-day trek.

You have to be in really good shape to hike this trail. At points along the way, you will be 12,000 feet above sea level—and when you cross Dead Woman's Pass, you will be at around 13,800 feet!

If you plan to visit Machu Picchu, you will need to keep an eye on the weather. The rainy season is between October and April. The dry season—the most popular season for tourists—is between May and September.

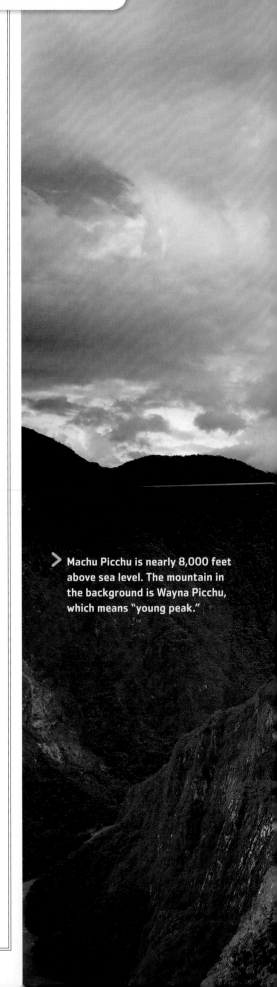

Machu Picchu is nearly 8,000 feet above sea level. The mountain in the background is Wayna Picchu, which means "young peak."

▲ Stones laid by the Inca guide hikers along the Inca Trail. It is one of the most popular hiking trails in South America.

A llama looks over the Central Plaza at Machu Picchu.

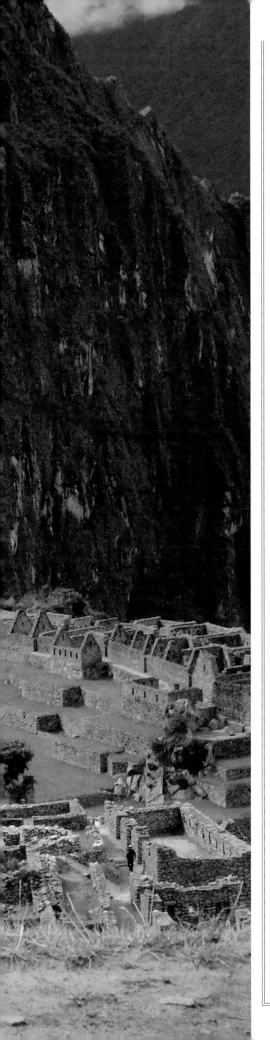

Mysterious Mountain City

When you visit a new place, it's good to learn a little history about it first. Machu Picchu was built around 1450. The Inca left no written records, so historians and archaeologists—those who study ancient cultures by looking at what the people left behind—came up with theories about why Machu Picchu was built. One theory was that it served a sacred, or religious, function; another was that it was a "lost city" where Inca rulers hid after the Spanish arrived.

Today, archaeologists believe that Machu Picchu was built as a retreat for the emperor Pachacuti (pah-chah-KOO-tee)—a place where he could "get away" from the demands of his rule. Machu Picchu was abandoned in the early 1500s, before the Spanish conquest. The Spanish had a habit of destroying important sites after conquering a culture, but Machu Picchu remained intact—largely because the Spanish never found it.

Machu Picchu sat undisturbed for several hundred years. Then, in 1911, a man from Yale University named Hiram Bingham was led by a Peruvian guide to a maze of jungle-covered walls. He cleared away some of the thick vegetation that hid the buildings and revealed the true genius of the city. Bingham took thousands of photographs and mapped the different parts of the site.

Hundreds of archaeologists have studied Machu Picchu since Bingham. They, along with Bingham, have uncovered the advanced techniques the Inca used to build the walls and waterworks, revealing why Machu Picchu is truly one of the most interesting places in the world.

Hitting the Highlights

When you enter Machu Picchu, you will notice that it has two main sections: the Agricultural Section, where the Inca farmed, and the Urban Section, where they lived. The Agricultural Section includes the terraces where the Inca grew crops. It also contains a cemetery and a guardhouse.

In the Urban Section, the Inca built the emperor's residence near the first of a series of fountains. This meant the Inca with the highest rank would have access to the purest water that flowed through the city. The Central Plaza runs through the middle of Machu Picchu. It sits above the section where workers lived and below temples and places where **rituals**, or religious ceremonies, were carried out. The Temple of the Sun and the Royal Tomb are also located in the Urban Section.

Throughout Machu Picchu, you can see that the Inca shaped stones without using complex tools. They did not use mortar, a cement-like material, to hold stones together; instead, they sculpted each large brick to fit tightly with others. Finally, their buildings had roofs made of thatch, or grasses and plant materials, to keep out sun and rain.

⌃ The granite terraces at Machu Picchu were built from the base of the mountain up. Terraces such as these in the Agricultural Section gave the Inca flat spaces to grow crops.

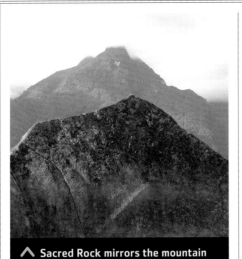

∧ Sacred Rock mirrors the mountain behind it. It shows the Inca's respect for nature.

∧ These stones fit tightly together. Even a piece of paper cannot slide through the cracks between them.

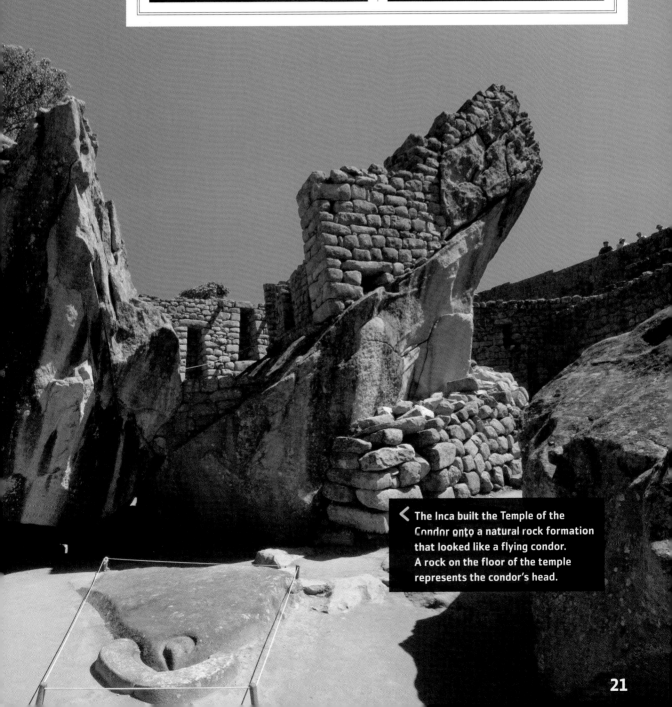

< The Inca built the Temple of the Condor onto a natural rock formation that looked like a flying condor. A rock on the floor of the temple represents the condor's head.

21

Salt Ponds and Circle Terraces

Machu Picchu is fascinating, but it isn't the only Inca site you can visit. The Urubamba Valley is full of many other interesting places to see.

The Inca harvested salt by building terraces to catch water from a **saline**, or salty, stream. The salt ponds at Las Salinas (sah-LEE-nahs) are still in operation today. Water from a saline stream above the terraces flows into more than 1,000 small ponds. In the dry season, water evaporates and workers harvest the salt that remains.

Ollantaytambo (ah-lon-tay-TAHM-boh) is a mountain village high above the Urubamba River. It has been continuously inhabited since the 1200s. Ollantaytambo served as an Inca **fortress**, or military fort, and it was one place where the Inca successfully fought off the Spanish during the conquest.

The circle terraces at Moray (mohr-AY) were built in three enormous pits. Temperatures varied significantly from the bottom to the top, so the Inca could experiment with which crops grew best at certain temperatures.

⌃ The Inca used these circle terraces for farming experiments.

< Find the people in the photo to get an idea of how large these salt ponds are.

My Inca Adventure

"It's a breathtaking place!" says Brian Nehlsen. In 2009, he visited the Urubamba Valley and toured Inca sites. Here is his account of the trip.

On the first day, I toured Machu Picchu. I arrived by bus at 5:30 in the morning and took some terrific photographs. The next day I went to Ollantaytambo. I was impressed by the water management system there. A mountain stream flows down into specially built canals—and it is still flowing today. On my third day, I visited Las Salinas and Moray. At Las Salinas, I marveled at how the Inca harvested so much salt from such a tiny stream. I bought some salt candy at the site. At Moray, a short distance from Las Salinas, I walked to the bottom of the terraces. I wondered, "How did the Inca build these nearly perfect circles?" I had a lot of fun in the Urubamba Valley. If I had the chance, I would definitely go back!

Check In What features of the Inca sites demonstrate Inca skills?

23

HIGH-ALTITUDE
Archaeology

by Andrea Alter

Thanks to a field of study called high-altitude archaeology, we know a lot about the Inca. **Archaeology** is the study of how people lived in the past. High-altitude archaeologists learn about how people lived in high altitudes long ago by studying artifacts they have left behind.

One challenge for high-altitude archaeologists is getting to the places they want to study. They have to be good hikers—even mountain climbers—to go to work. Once they reach their study sites, which can be 10,000 to 20,000 feet above sea level, oxygen is less plentiful. Lack of oxygen can cause altitude sickness, or being tired and nauseous. So, high-altitude archaeologists must adapt to "thin air" conditions and develop the endurance and strength of athletes.

Archaeology at high altitudes also includes the risk of avalanches, rockslides, snowstorms, and falls. Winds can be fierce 10,000 feet above sea level, and temperatures can suddenly drop very low. To stay safe and warm, high-altitude archaeologists must use the right mountaineering gear.

High-altitude archaeologists study many different cultures around the world. In the Rocky Mountains in the western United States, archaeologist Chris Morgan researches prehistoric settlements in Wyoming's Wind River mountain range. Archaeologist Johan Reinhard works in the mountains of Peru, and Constanza Ceruti works in Argentina. Both study the Inca in South America, and both work with National Geographic.

High-altitude archaeologists work in mountain ranges all over the world. The Wind River Range is a mountain range in Wyoming. It stretches along the Continental Divide in the western United States.

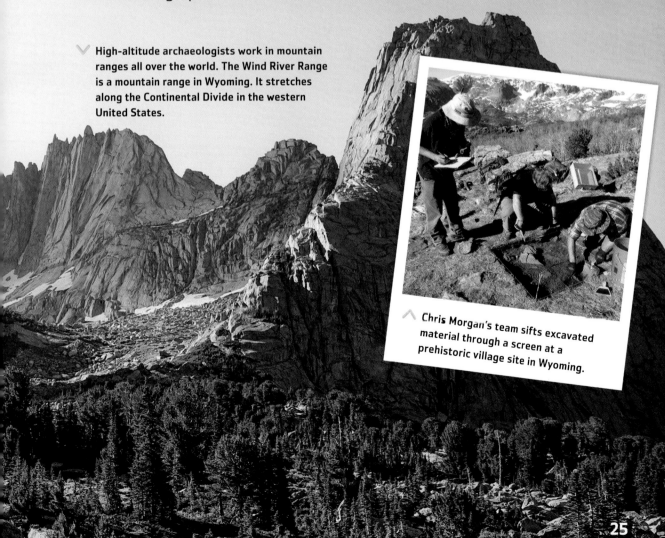

Chris Morgan's team sifts excavated material through a screen at a prehistoric village site in Wyoming.

Johan Reinhard Makes a Discovery

Johan Reinhard is a man who is not afraid to conquer a mountain. He has made more than 200 treks to high **summits**, or tops of mountains.

Reinhard is a high-altitude archaeologist and a National Geographic Explorer. Reinhard's early interest in detective stories and mountain climbing prepared him for his life's work: studying the sacred rituals of mountain people. He began his fieldwork studying cultures in the Himalaya of Nepal. Since then, he's spent three decades learning about mountain people in the Andes.

In 1995, Reinhard and his climbing partner, Miguel Zárate, were hiking along a mountain ridge on Nevado Ampato (ahm-PAH-toh), a 20,700-foot mountain in Peru. The two noticed something unusual on the slope below them, so they hiked down to it and realized it was a frozen Inca mummy! It was an extraordinary find.

> Johan Reinhard has discovered more than 50 Inca ritual sites. Here, Reinhard and his team hike an icy ridge on Nevado Ampato.

JOHAN REINHARD read about explorers when he was a boy and decided to live a life of adventure. Although he is a famous high-altitude archaeologist, his first archaeological job was underwater. He studied Roman shipwrecks in the Mediterranean Sea. Reinhard has also put his diving skills to use in the Andes. He has explored beneath Lake Titicaca, a lake high in the mountains.

Only a few frozen mummies have ever been discovered on high Andean summits, and this one was especially well preserved. The body of the mummy, a female, had been frozen for hundreds of years. Medical experts used x-rays and chemical analysis to determine her age and health before she died.

Near the mummy, Reinhard found gold figurines, cloth bags, and pottery used for burial rituals, which confirmed that Nevado Ampato was a sacred Inca site. Reinhard's discovery opened the door to understanding much more about Inca rituals and encouraged him to continue searching high in the Andes.

Sub-zero Andean temperatures preserved the mummy Johan Reinhard and Miguel Zárate discovered.

Constanza Ceruti Fulfills Her Dream

Some people are lucky enough to know exactly what they want to be when they grow up. Constanza Ceruti, a National Geographic Explorer, is one of them. By the age of 14, she knew she wanted to be a high-altitude archaeologist. Ceruti grew up in Argentina and now specializes in sacred mountain sites of the Inca. She knows that not everyone would be excited to spend weeks at a time camping in the high mountains, enduring frostbite, blizzards, lightning, and long hikes up and down from basecamp. However, she loves what she does for a living.

The mummies Ceruti discovered are at a museum in Salta, Argentina. They are displayed in refrigerated, low-oxygen cases.

In 1999, Ceruti was working in Argentina at the summit of Mount Llullaillaco (yoo-yay-AH-koh) with Johan Reinhard and his team. At 22,000 feet above sea level, it is the world's highest archaeological site. Conditions on the summit were brutal. It was very cold, a snowstorm was bearing down, and the winds were whipping with great force. The team was excavating Inca ruins, hopeful to find evidence of Inca mountain rituals—or even another Inca mummy. Not only did they discover one mummy; they found three!

Leaving the summit, the team had to be sure the mummies stayed frozen. If they thawed, scientists would not be able to study them. The team carried the mummies down the steep mountain quickly and carefully. Once at the base, they placed the mummies in dry ice and took them to a laboratory where they could be studied. After Ceruti and Reinhard studied them, the mummies were put on display at a museum in Argentina.

CONSTANZA CERUTI was born in Buenos Aires, Argentina. As a high-altitude archaeologist, she has climbed more than 100 mountains higher than 16,500 feet. Though she has scaled mountains all over the world, her heart is in the Andes Mountains. There she combines her love of mountain climbing with her enthusiasm for learning more about the Inca.

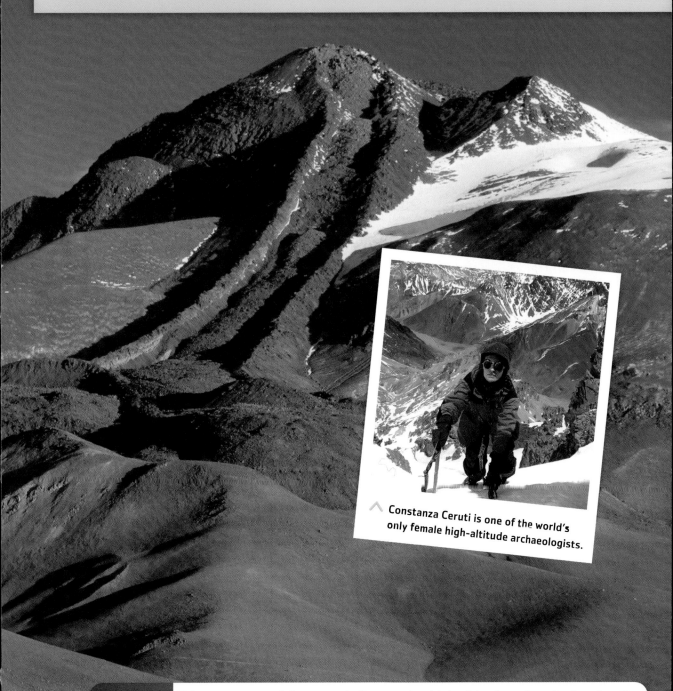

Constanza Ceruti is one of the world's only female high-altitude archaeologists.

Check In What are some of the main challenges that high-altitude archaeologists face?

Inca Artifacts

by Lily Tucker

When high-altitude archaeologists such as Johan Reinhard and Constanza Ceruti return from a dig, they often have **artifacts**, or items made by humans, to show. Lucky for us, some of these artifacts are displayed in museums, where we can learn what the Inca valued and how they lived.

The Inca treasured the gold and silver that they mined from rich deposits in the Andes. Spanish conquistadors heard tales of these riches. They were not disappointed when they reached the Inca Empire. During and after the conquest, the Spanish **looted**, or stole, these treasures from the Inca and melted them down. Fortunately, some artifacts survived.

> Gold llama, 15th century

< Gold female figurine, 15th century

Numerous small gold and silver figurines have been found at Inca burial sites. Many of these wear miniature woven wraps, fastened with a gold or silver pin. Gold and silver statues of llamas have also been found at burial sites. Both the ceremonial use of precious metals and the wealth they brought to the Inca and their conquerors demonstrate how important gold and silver were in the Inca Empire.

Some Inca artifacts tell us about past rituals. Archaeologists have learned about Inca rituals through the vessels, or containers, the Inca created and used. One vessel, called an *aryballos* (ar-uh-BY-yohs), was used for storage. It held *chicha* (CHEE-chah), a beverage made from corn. During religious ceremonies, the Inca filled an aryballos with chicha. They poured the chicha on the ground to ask the gods for a good growing season.

< Aryballos, 15th century

> Quipu, 15th century

The Inca used a system of knotted counting cords called *quipus* (KEE-poos) to record information. The word *quipu* means "knot" in Quechua. The placement and colors of knots on quipus had specific values and helped the Inca count crops, livestock, and weapons. Quipus also kept track of dates and events. Quipus were created and read by trained Inca workers.

Check In   What can we learn about the Inca from the artifacts they left behind?

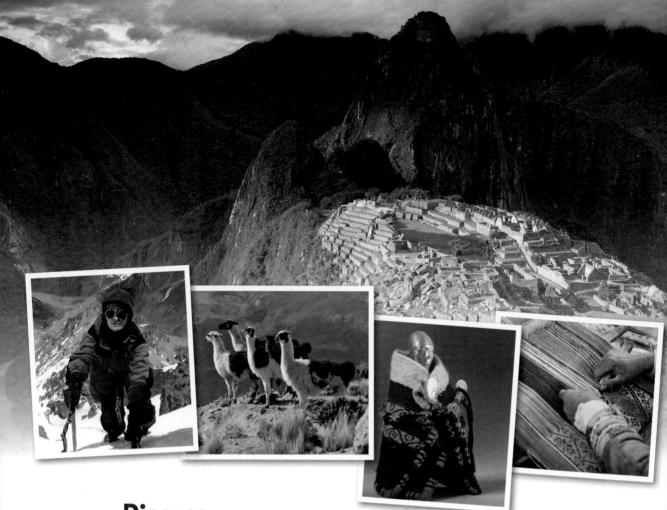

Discuss

1. What do you think connects the five pieces you read in this book? What makes you think that?

2. How did the Inca build such a powerful and amazing empire? What caused the empire to come to an end?

3. Describe how llamas were important to the Inca and how they are still valued by the Quechua.

4. How have high-altitude archaeologists contributed to our knowledge of the Inca?

5. What do you still wonder about the Inca? What would you like to learn more about?